W9-CME-614

Math Around Us

Measuring in the Garden

Tracey Steffora

Heinemann Library
Chicago, Illinois

www.capstonepub.com

Visit our website to find out more information about Heinemann-Raintree books.

To order:

☎ Phone 800-747-4992

💻 Visit www.capstonepub.com
to browse our catalog and order online.

© 2011 Heinemann Library
an imprint of Capstone Global Library, LLC
Chicago, Illinois

All rights reserved. No part of this publication may be reproduced or transmitted in any form or by any means, electronic or mechanical, including photocopying, recording, taping, or any information storage and retrieval system, without permission in writing from the publisher.

Edited by Rebecca Rissman, Tracey Steffora, and Catherine Veitch
Designed by Joanna Hinton-Malivoire
Picture research by Elizabeth Alexander
Production by Victoria Fitzgerald
Originated by Capstone Global Library Ltd
Printed and bound in the United States of America,
North Mankato, MN 052013   007422RP

15 14 13
10 9 8 7 6 5 4

Library of Congress Cataloging-in-Publication Data
Steffora, Tracey.
  Measuring in the garden / Tracey Steffora.
    p. cm.—(Math around us)
  Includes bibliographical references and index.
  ISBN 978-1-4329-4926-6 (hc)—ISBN 978-1-4329-4934-1
(pb) 1. Gardens—Juvenile literature. 2. Measurement—
Juvenile literature. I. Title.
  SB457.S84 2011
  530.8—dc22   2010030770

Acknowledgments
The author and publisher are grateful to the following for permission to reproduce photographs: © Capstone Publishers p. 22 (Karon Dubke); Alamy pp. 7 (© Victor Watts), 19 (© Robert Harrison); Corbis p. 5 (© Yi Lu); iStockphoto pp. 6 (© Elena Elisseeva), 14 (© Carmen Martínez Banús); Photolibrary pp. 13 (Jochen Tack/imagebroker.net), 18 (Garden Picture Library), 20 (Photos Lamontagne/Garden Picture Library), 21 (Michael Freeman/Red Cover); Shutterstock pp. 4 (© Sternstunden), 6 inset (© Christophe Testi), 8 (© Vitaly Romanovich), 9 (© Monkey Business Images), 11 (© Kenneth Sponsler), 10 (© Gina Smith), 12 (© a40757), 15 (© Joe Gough), 16 (© Kokhanchikov), 17 (© master stock), 23 glossary – earthworm (© Kokhanchikov), 23 glossary – soil (© Monkey Business Images), 23 glossary – temperature (© Christophe Testi).

Cover photograph of a girl watering a plant reproduced with permission of Shutterstock (© Monkey Business Images). Back cover photograph of a vegetable garden reproduced with permission of iStockphoto (© Carmen Martínez Banús).

We would like to thank Nancy Harris, Dee Reid, and Diana Bentley for their assistance in the preparation of this book.

Every effort has been made to contact copyright holders of material reproduced in this book. Any omissions will be rectified in subsequent printings if notice is given to the publisher.

Contents

Gardens

Many things grow in gardens.

We can help gardens grow.

How Warm?

thermometer

We measure temperature to know when to plant.

Plants grow in warm weather.
We plant in spring and summer.

How Much?

Plants grow in soil.

Large pots hold more soil.

soil

Small pots hold less soil.

water lily

Plants need water.

Some plants need more water.

cactus

Some plants need less water.

Plants need space.

Some plants need more space.

Some plants need less space.

How Tall?

beans

lettuce

Plants can be different sizes. The beans are taller than the lettuce.

The red flowers are taller than the
white flowers.

How Long?

Earthworms live in soil.

Earthworms are good for soil.

Which worm is longer?

Which worm is shorter?

How Heavy?

Some gardens have rocks.

Rocks can be small and light.

Rocks can be big and heavy.

Gardens Everywhere

This garden is on a wall.

This garden is on a roof.

Planting Seeds

Plants need space to grow. Use your hand to measure a space between each seed or plant.

Picture Glossary

 **earthworm** a worm that lives in damp earth or soil

 **soil** a loose part of the earth in which plants grow

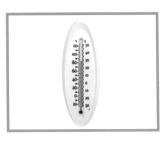 **temperature** a measure of how warm or cold something is

Index

Notes to Parents and Teachers

Before reading

Young children first begin to understand measurement through comparisons. Provide children with opportunities to experience and use vocabulary such as more and less, longer and shorter, heavier and lighter, or bigger and smaller. Discuss how we measure and compare things in our environment all the time, even if we are not using formal measuring tools such as rulers or scales.

After reading

• Plant seeds with children, utilizing vocabulary of size, weight, height, and volume.

• Take a walk in your neighborhood or community and look for gardens. These might be found in a park or in a sidewalk container. Discuss how plants can grow in many places and discuss the important role they play in our world (supplying food, oxygen, beauty, etc.)